AF259509

The Raven Prayers

Poems from a Mind Between Faith and Doubt

William F. Burk

Copyright © 2021 by William F. Burk

All rights reserved.

No portion of this book may be reproduced in any form without written permission from the publisher or author, except as permitted by U.S. copyright law.

To my dearest friends, who talked me through 2016.

Introduction

This is the second publication of this volume. The first, The Lonely Hymns: Poems and Reflections, never really fit into the vision I had for it. Thusly, this redirection of the volume perhaps captures the context of the pieces a bit better. This context, of course, was my struggle through a psychotic depression whilst battling bipolar 1 disorder in 2016. About ninety percent of the poems you just read were written during that time. I have collected them to highlight my struggles with existence, the will to carry on, and faith and doubt during this period. I hope that perhaps these poems will make you contemplate some of these subjects and give you a look into the mind of this mental illness.

Contents

Jacob's Ladder

The music muses

me to sleep, and

I fall into

dormancy,

drifting toward a door

through which

I dream of aether.

Symphonic drowning——

I court my thoughts

spiraling above

my head,

climbing up

Jacob's Ladder. They

come and go,

dreaming of long

ago——of TV shows and

times in the woods——

searching for that place

I cannot find on earth.

But I move ever slowly,

gladly through that door of aether,

where the sun doesn't

hinder snow,

and I know I will

be there,

and see that dreamworld soon.

Spots of Silver

The stars

above sit,

alone, hanging

in spots of silver.

We sat alone,

and watched

their glow,

guided by what

emotions were there.

Black canvas—with holes

of light, we wonder

what is real. Beyond

the haze is a

stroke of luck,

and wonder why

we came to feel

that way.

4:04 AM

Four-O!-four,

I want no more

of the things that

life gives me.

I simply sigh

to life, passing by,

and the growing sense

of futility.

Please Disregard the Clocks Inside of the Stratosphere

Slow songs,

to the sound

of disregard,

spill into the

starry night,

and make

him realize

his insignificance.

Planes

overhead,

with purrs

of adventure,

Beginning.

Ending.

Starting over...

hold your head

lower, and

smell the cold air.

Breathe.

Feel that?

Alive.

Stand, and look at the sky,

for two billion light-years,

the specs of light

at the end of your sight

detail, decorate

how small every

argument, and

all you've

achieved

under the

stratosphere.

The fears he held

were simply small,

then it came to him,

as a spectrum of

clockwork,

a fluidity...

...and regaining

sanity, he realized:

Maybe the worry of worth

wasn't worth the worry.

Difference

All is but

a moment—

within a vague

plane...

of destinies

which are never

the same.

The Socrates Sonnet

The moon shines sadly as Socrates dies,

shining down the glass of hemlock and death,

the shameless man to curse the gods, he cries.

He speaks from his mind; he speaks without breath.

To him—to see—the truth in brazen light,

to run from the things that tear him apart,

knowing that "to know" is but a failed blight,

"To death, I've no fear," he speaks from his heart,

"To say, to say, 'I will be; I will be!'

I will spite the cold of death's frigid frost!"

To Plato's sight, a grand apology,

viewing lunacy dancing, his eyes lost.

The man, the man, the manic man dances—

smiling—as he scorns Wisdom's advances.

The Socrates Haiku

Socrates to drink

a poison, cold as winter,

while the asters wilt.

Soon and Sudden (or, Reading Ecclesiastes)

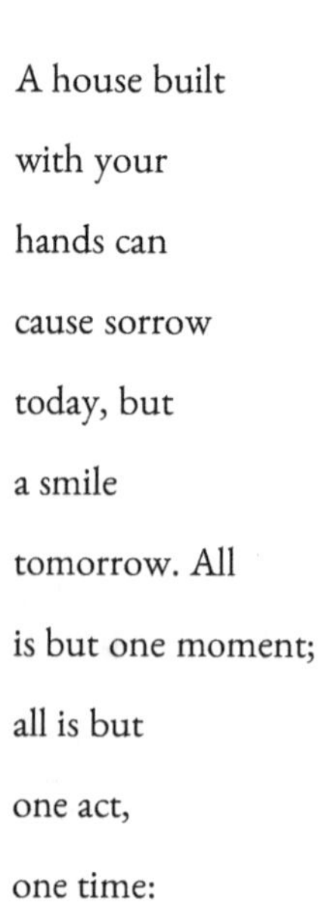

A house built

with your

hands can

cause sorrow

today, but

a smile

tomorrow. All

is but one moment;

all is but

one act,

one time:

to cry——

to laugh——

to live——

to die——

all under

the sun, all

under the

moon.

And slowly,

we come to terms,

and know

that life

is utterly

soon and sudden...

the fly watches he

The Fly

darts across

the wall,

unknowing of

what it sees.

The seas

of emotion——

a fragile

dance——

that fly upon

the wall, hears

its name.

Bears its

name. And

sees all it

can.

The floating bug,

he so disregards————

wisped upon the wall,

perhaps it

hears him————

"Fly! Fly!

Tell me what

you see!"

"A maniac!" he

screams, "A

maniac, is he!"

"You see?" I say,

"You see from the wall?"

"I see! I

see! From here on

the wall. He dances

round and round!"

"Fly! Oh, fly!

Why does he

move? A sea of

passion, kept

like sands on

the beach!"

And thus fly returns:

"I see! I

see! That manic

man dances...

Screaming!

 Singing!

As if the world

had crashed around him!"

Barbershop Blues

Postmodern——

in magazines, with

a pixie cut on the

front. Barbershop——the

Stylist cuts bits

of natural to

conform to

corporate.

You can't look

like a wild man

and climb the

mountains of

the ladder

at the office.

He sits in silence

as the Stylist——

she spits gossip,

and snips away...

Dim Lit Espresso

Coffee shop, with

dim lit,

dark espresso,

consistent highs and

lows———college kid,

with a

book or two.

I too, far from

my last semester,

sit in the room,

typing away.

Maybe one day,

he will move on

from the books,

and into the fantasy.

The Monk, the Book, and the Sunset

The monk's face

was ridden with

the crevasses of

withering time.

Serenely, he sat

nose deep in

a book he'd

continually been

unable to finish.

Many of life's errands

had swiveled him to and

fro and distracted

him. Now an old man,

he lay on his cot and

turned his eyes to the tome.

Dusk was fast approaching, and

he knew that

time was nigh.

The sun sank

on the horizon

of the ancient

earth, as did the heart

of the seemingly ancient

monk. Wholeheartedly,

he focused

his gaze upon the

ink of the letters,

slowly fading

into shadow.

Three times he

had tried:

once as a boy,

another as a youth,

and now,

once as an elder.

Tearing up

at the dimming light,

he closed the book, and

lay his head

upon the straw...

Perhaps tomorrow,

if tomorrow comes.

Aspiration (or, Hugging Luna)

Life is

passing

by like sand,

sifting through

a silky glass figure that

resembles the number eight——

aspiring through the crux

to reach the bottom...

Fleeting,

yet we still reach outward——

to hug the moon.

so, like, that grenade's not real, right?

The sadness

and

destruction,

a reprimand to

concurrency

of the heart's gaze

upon the moon

and how it glows,

illuminating the night.

Whitewash——

the color of

bleach, detox,

over a black canvas

that beats in your chest

and makes you

walk and sing,

evergreen,

a view of

bias to the

beauty in

the eye

of the beholder.

Hold her,

and and take her

hand, as

life slips away

unto the bottom

of a vial of sand.

Suffering is

a grand scheme:

to kill you,

or make you

breathe, with

the night in your veins,

which beats to the

sound of

rain: tumultuous,

a fantastic display of

affection, to grab the thorns

despite the blood...

I'll tell you this:

what I know,

that love is

holding a grenade

and praying it's a dud.

Flight of the Silverbird

Silver bird,

with wings of steel,

graces the through

the sky. One would

even think

that man should

not be able

to fly in such

a way.

Eyes of Antares

Holy stark,

intimate stars———

falling from

the sky.

He looks

above, then

looks at her

eyes———those

hazel eyes———

and sees a

universe he'd

not seen before.

For just

as vast

are those

eyes as

the cosmic

dust around

Antares, illuminated———

cast into

a beating

heart, a

pulse.

Never before...

had he seen

such a depth

than in those

eyes.

Starlet Mind

Like sunlit

beams——the moon

alive——casts over

the hearts

where lovers strive.

Twenty-one:

a rarity———

she fell in

love with the

moon and how it

shines: bright

in life———a starlet

mind.

Lunar kiss:

she says

goodnight. She

reaches out,

as the waves do,

with captured

conviction of wide-

eyed avail.

She's a wild

spirit———

and more alive

than you

or I.

She Told Me (or, at Fourteen)

Lyra told me

she'd slit her

wrists at the age

of fourteen.

I knew,

if she died,

the snow would

still fall in the

winter———————

the sun would

still rise—————

the moon still

glow.

But if she died,

time would stand

still; the world

would quiet

to hear the drop

of a pin.

The sun

would rise,

yet not shine.

The moon would

glow, but lose its

mystery.

The snow would

fall, yet cease

its glitter...

True that time

would stand still————

and all fail to

luster.

And I knew, when

she told me———

at the age

of fourteen———

if she dies,

all of the world's

wonder would

die with her.

Lively Rhythms

What is it that you see in

the brazen skyline? In the sight

of the sun, that grand flame that

dances upon the blue irises that

hold it high?

The sun sets, but,

your blue eyes still

dance in lively rhythms.

The Drowning Prayer

Peter, why did you

look away? Did the

ghosts of the sea

call you by name?

From the storm,

I see your heart,

that glows in

brilliant black———

speckled in

salt to preserve

the world, unlike

the ones who pray

aloud.

Take my hand,

Peter; take my hand,

and I shall call you

someday from

the ground.

Flowers in the Tears of December

Peter, why did you

look away? Did the

ghosts of the sea

call you by name?

From the storm,

I see your heart,

that glows in

brilliant black———

speckled in

salt to preserve

the world, unlike

the ones who pray

aloud.

Take my hand,

Peter; take my hand,

and I shall call you

someday from

the ground.

The World Sleeps for Solomon

The world, it

sleeps as Solomon

commands to cut the

child in half, a

wisdom to which

the mother screams

in sudden sincerity———

an awakening, as the

moon stirs the

demons of the

sea———

the world———

it sleeps, as she

lulls the child.

As it cries,

as it cries,

as it cried for

the embrace of

the wise man.

A calling for sorrow.

A calling for grief.

It cries away,

but the mother, she

smiles,

as her world

sleeps...

For You Alone

Twinkling lights

above cast down

upon the groves

of Eden———

careless, as

Adam hums a

tune, the

Fruit hangs among

the tree———

loneliness,

the cost of

a rib, to

name her

Eve————

and love

her,

like the

rain will

kiss your face...

as if it

were all

for you alone.

Strive

Why does

man strive

against time

only to realize

that he missed

the point?

At death's

door is where

man ultimately

sees the true——

the true, full

picture——

the glimpse

of what life

is, and what he

missed...

Only at the

end does

man realize

the gravity

that time

was fleeting...

The Song of Thomas

Among———amid

the disciple's whirling

gaze,

a man sit before

him——

before us now,

risen from the

grave, filled three

days from the

present————

with scars

upon his wrist.

A scar sits

along his side for

the foolish one to

touch and say: "It's

you! It's you!

for they said you

died, that they

took you, wrapped you

and laid you cold

below, but

you sit here now————

against belief, and

watch us all sing songs

of fairy tales, or

though we thought,

of the man we once

called master——

called rabbi——

our Messiah——

who died alone, and

caused us all to weep,

but now you

stand, and sing

with us, like the

way you did before.

We sing together,

and laugh, and

cry,

with the man we

now call God———

who walks again

from hanging high

and placed Death

within his grave..."

The Rugged Nazarene

Oh I did see that rugged Nazarene,

that he was the messiah come to be.

Upon a glance nothing was to be seen.

Yet he had seen all that was and had been,

was God and man, in perfect harmony.

Oh, did I see that rugged Nazarene!

He was coming to the world's greatest scene,

on that faithful advent of Calvary.

Upon a glance, nothing was to be seen.

And so he went to pray in gardens green,

for the Father's plan of his destiny;

oh, did I see that rugged Nazarene!

And as the Prophets of Old had foreseen,

that he was to be hung upon a tree.

Upon a glance, nothing was to be seen.

They did not know that God did intervene,

that this man was to die for those like we.

Oh, did I see that rugged Nazarene!

Upon a glance, nothing was to be seen.

Earth to Luther

Delusions of grandeur—————
a great grenade of change.
Wild abandon——leave the house,
and walk on four feet——
catch your faltering humility,

and sit with me
on the edge of the pew——
back row, we
stand alone,
as the ghost of Calvin
spills out——fills the room.

Earth to Luther! You
were a heretic once.
My idol, now I see,

that stylish men in pews

are alike the tombstones outside:

cold, but not dead...

for they were never alive to begin with.

Candlelit Euangelion

Inside a church so dark,

there was a candle——

light that

reached my heart.

It reminds me

of that message

on Christmas Day,

that the angels sang,

to shepherds:

"On this day,

the King,

the Reason, divine,

He draws near!

He draws near!"

Of Marvell

Walking,

with umbrella in hand.

No resistance

to winters tears.

A man of sixty-eight

strides along

the rows of stones.

Memories,

etched into letters

and numbers of

an allotted time,

serendipity,

of youthful days

gone by——

passed away——

and soon he will too.

He stares at the grave...

...and wonders why God has cursed him so.

Trilogies

She reads

trilogies:

Lord of the Rings,

for the fifth time

since last December.

She likes the hobbits,

their careful ways,

thinks the elves almost

as mysterious as

Gandalf himself,

and wonders if Gollum

looked the same in Tolkien's

mind as he did in the movies.

Cinema was a

visual escape,

unfurled and over.

Done with.

Right now,

she sits silently and

stares at the floor,

upon her life in the

broken, jagged glass

of a picture frame.

She sits alone and

weeps to God:

"Take me to Middle-Earth!

Take me to Middle-Earth..."

Un-Apart

Walking a distance

with a cock-eyed

gaze, wearily

set on the dispersing

clouds that

revealed the

resilience of

the sun's rays...

...and at

that moment

he realized

that he and

the sky

weren't so far

apart.

The Blue Blood and the Ugandan Boy

Pearl——

a gem in a valley,

as Churchill described it,

a description on point,

as I would testify—

despite my sweat.

I was a sight——

Mzungu: white

guy who "runs in circles,"

riding over the chaotic pot holes.

A landscape with

no welfare

to the vendors on the streets

while Bastille beat drums in my ears,

a tether to the privilege of home.

On arrival,

I heard a Mosque—

on speaker-phone,

bellowing five pillars

out into the streets,

across from the school,

where I spoke to the child.

Mzungu——

a louder curiosity than

the call to prayer.

Mission work—

I told him

a mute salvation

as he rubs my wrist to

test the myth, and

see my "blue blood."

This is

what history has given him:

Imperial inferiority——

contrived. Smoke and

mirrors.

This young boy

in the slums. To him

I am simply "Mzungu"——

a reminder of the pervasive regimes

his family talks about:

I am the one with blue in his veins.

And I still wonder,

to this day,

what he would have done,

if I had sliced my hand

open, just to show him

that oxidation makes us all red.

Calling Lazarus

God cried for Lazarus————
the man in the grave,
wrapped in spiced cloth.

Oh, Mary! Oh, Martha!
Your brother sinks to
Sheol, while the Reason
weeps aside you————
beside you.

He sits in tears for a man
he loved as the moon
fills the daytime sky.

A man he loves—————

he commands from

the fangs of Sheol:

"Dear Lazarus! My

dearest Lazarus!

Dine with me once

once more! Laugh

with me once again!

Lazarus! Come out!"

And Sheol set him free.

A Surprising Stranger (or, Yahweh in the Wilderness)

I walked away

from a coffee

shop counter,

without saying

goodbye to the

god who worked

There———

I walked among

the Wilderness where

a Stranger sounded

like a messenger of

Reason———

A vigil of hope from

the pains of the

World———

He talked to me

and showed me His

Face———

And thus I sang

as I sat with God,

and drank black espresso:

"You are not the God of

my father, my brother, my people..."

And thus I sang:

"You are Yahweh———

and you are not what I expected."

The Day Death Died.

I saw

the Nazarene

climb the stalk

of the stairs

to the top

of the temple

to be

tempted by

Satan, who

said, "I will

give you everything,

just live for me."

Repent, and

thou shalt be

saved: an epitaph

to the epitome

of unfairness,

that man might

see God on a

tree———

hung there

for all but God

the Father to see:

"Eli, Eli, Lama Sabachthani!"

Forsaken to hang for me.

Hell splits open from

within a crown

of thorns, to be

worn by the King

of Peace——the King

now damned,

and now he

lives again—-

no body to be

found dead,

but risen: alive and

Well!

Mary! Mary!

What do you say

to the angels

at the grave?

Do you weep?

Do you cheer?

Your Jesus is

alive and well.

She sat there,

and through tears

she said: "My

King has risen,

and Death is dead."

The Raven Prayer

The birds

will gaze

upon the

stars and

wonder why

they dance.

The sky

above, so

dark and

speckled——

they lust

to feel the

air.

Oh, Man

Above, what

do you see

when you

watch the

ravens fly?

Is it joyous?

Do you

weep? When you

let the birds

take wing——and

do you care

for the flocks

of birds as

much as you do

me?

Oh Man Above———

if you are

above———do you

see us scurry

about? Tell

me now, what

is aloof in your

mind? What

do you think

about the stars

as you call their

names when they

fall or die?

And are we

the stars

that died ago,

and does our

light reach you?

Do you see each

of us here,

striving to-

and-fro———and

what do you think

of our lights————

the ones that

died long

ago?

Oh, Man Above,

I must admit————

I watch the

birds as I

gaze upon the

stars, and I

wonder why

we dance.

The Train Tracks

The train tracks

shield the rain

from the man

who lies beneath

them. The railroad sits,

worn, deserted———

a ghost town———

a relic of a time,

passed by,

its mysterious

paths to elsewhere——

forgotten——

but the man

is happy for

his ancient abode.

He is lost below

its rusty roof,

but, for now,

he is merely thankful

to be out of the rain.

The Protest

Curved———

an alignment

over steaming

pavement——

from the

weeping of

the heavens,

of one man

turned against

another——hands

held without

avail——a message

to be learned

like the ones

before——a halt

as car engines

roar——and exhaust

dissipates into

the air around.

We are but dust,

and dust is

our destiny——

but Cain still

kills Abel,

and over what?

And still——

the lines align

perpendicular.

O foolish man,

when will you

see?

That we are

all dust,

a blot in time———

why, man,

can you not

get along?

Why, Cain? Why

did you kill

your brother?

His blood cries out

from the soil...

"Why, O why,

must dust

slay dust?"

Jupiter for the King

Men from the orient are

following a

western star: Jupiter,

the most majestic

planet——a herald——

for a child——

a king——

much greater than Augustus.

Angels hark to

shepherds in the

field: "Rejoice, God is

coming near!"

With propitiation

for the sins

of the world,

bathed in

blood, baptized, and

a curtain torn.

A new covenant——

a promise kept——

for Emmanuel

was born, and

in a virgin's lap

slept the King

of Kings——

Logos: the

Reason, wrapped

in flesh, and God

became a man

to save his

harlot bride from

her sins.

The Garden We Call Green

Oh, my friend,

what do you see

in the garden we call

green? Has God

lost his way in his

travels? Why

do you sit and watch

the stars, and do you

wish to leave——

behind the pain,

behind the strife,

of the world

hopelessly set

in motion.

Oh, my friend,

what do you see

in the garden

we call green?

A Tree of Life?

An apple red?

A snake beneath

the trees?

If you had

one chance

to speak to Eve

(if you believe in Eve)

what would you

say (as the snake

climbs the tree)?

Would you tell her

your woes, or of

a God long gone,

that left us——

diseased.

Tell me, my friend,

what do you see

in that garden

we call green?

When Thomas Saw the Scars

We all have

crosses to be

nailed to. Three

nails and a cat

of nine tails———

I sit here in

sorrow.

40 days, or

something like

that: a savior

is about to leave.

Come again, you

thief. Helpless and

articulate, my

words pulse

from my monochrome

mind onto the page....

Thomas,

you idiot...

at least you got to see his scars....

Tilting

I left you,

my friend,

in the coils

of the telephone——

a landline.

I had to

go.

The white

filled my

mind, and

solitude

was the only

place I could

find that

rectified

the meaning

in the tears,

captivated.

I know I told

you we'd go

away, seek

the world———

find what

we want———

but it is

no more.

Delusions of grandeur!
I fell in love

with Don Quixote----

a madman like

me: he sees

the things

in dreams,

like I see

there too...

 to wake,

  away,

and wish

the dream

to be true—————

for within my

 shaking hands...

  my slobber...

   my tears...

I cry to God

to move the

stars———the

ones I look

at now, they

don't shine as

bright as

they used to...

but now,

I say,

like Quixote,

too: I watch

the stars

with my waking eyes,

and wish the

dream were

reality.

Manic Meltdown

Snap!

Bruce Banner:

no serendipity then,

with sudden asphyxiation

and eyes without inhibition——

evil twin.

Rage——

wild and unhindered,

wide bewildered eyes:

post-desirable happiness——

the mind tears itself apart.

You grin at the bathroom mirror

in eldritch epiphany:

the pump of

his pulse in your veins...

breathlessly——

you smile so hard

that it hurts...

Cornbread in the Shower

Socrates, you fool...

You eat cornbread

in the shower———with

a dizzy stance, and

no power. Socrates, you

fool————

a maniac———you are!

You think———therefore...?

Not too sure you even think?

What is "to think?"

I think for myself.

I think of thinking———

thinking

of thinking

of thinking

of thinking of

thinking————at 4 a.m.

To think, therefore be?———

Why, perhaps I be,

therefore I think...

I don't know.

Sleeping for a Year

I met

God once

in the salt

wrap of a

capsule.

Mercy made

of chemicals

contain characters

of sanity, sweeping

through my blood——

with songs of

solace. Mellow——

a multitude——

slipping through

the streets

of sanguine:

mesmerized,

with drowsy

effects.

I slept for

a year once.

And, in that time,

I saw God's mercy

in the pills I ate.

Bipolar Bear

A fractured mind

betwixt the seems

of barren fields

and fields of green.

The Precipice

Fade,

the Cheshire grin.

Biased mentality,

the foreboding

of reality grim.

The maniac,

lost inside his head

sits on the tail end.

Precipice,

with no sweet repose,

a transition——

from paradise to lost.

The grim realization

of life is that life

is, in reality, grim.

Anxious——

with a trembling voice

and heart fluttering,

a tension of conflict.

Carefully, the pen cries,

guided by a heavy hand

with a heavy pulse.

Sanity wrote her will——

and vexed the man she left.

Super-Joyed, Super-Serendipity

Detox.

Let it seep from

your skin,

utterly defiant,

follow it to the end.

Overjoyed——

with serendipity in hand:

torrential rambling:

dysentery of

the mind.

A head——

to be lost in, with

hallucinogenic happiness:

the destruction behind

a smile...

It's that grimace

we find so sweet

that haunts me...

and makes me sweat.

Hawkeyed Mania

Seemingly everlasting,

the wild

abandon——

with the eye

of a hawk,

bright as day...

who would have thought

those wild eyes

were sick...?

Zyprexa

The rain pelts

down in sounds

of systematic

symphonies

alluring to

the beckon

of rain clouds

and a foggy mind

tempted to

remain vigilant.

But eventually,

Zyprexa overcomes

the state of

being...

...awake...

Windowsill

Nothing justifies

your sadness;

nothing justifies

your woe.

You stand there

on the windowsill

and see others

come and go.

What is it

in that beating

chest of yours

that makes you

want to die?

With the same eyes

that you see dark with

are the ones that you see

life.

Why do you stand

on that windowsill

and look down below?

You know it is

a great fall,

but is it

really the way to go?

Perhaps if you

wait long enough

you will see better days.

Life is a mix of

things: the good and

the bad, and sometimes,

we see no way

when we are so sad.

Hard times come,

that is true, but

there is also joy,

and you should not

give up your life

when the dark

comes to destroy.

Think with me,

to times long gone,

when the sun shone

so bright. I tell you: clouds

will pass away,

and there will always

be light. Listen here,

and hear my words,

for right now

things seem lost,

but despite

what the darkness says,

it is not worth the cost.

Life is a mix of things:

of darkness and of light,

and though we go through

many trials, there will

always be more bright.

So I ask you now,

come off that windowsill

and lay down in your bed.

I know a lot has happened

and there are many things

in your head. But the

darkness is not true, you see,

no, the darkness is a lie,

and despite the mistakes

you've made, son,

you don't deserve to die.

The Box

Sheer emotion

sills his veins

with black.

Logic

spits flames

as a voice in his head.

He sits at the edge

and looks down below.

"Get up, young man

you don't want to go——

to spiral to the bottom.

For at the end of this emotion

lies only death,

but I'm going to tell you

you can make it not so.

You don't have sit,

at the edge of that ledge

like your perception tells you so.

Perhaps outside

the box you're in

the sun shines upon the snow.

Sure,

life is bleak,

and many come and

go, but outside of

that box you're in

the sun shines upon the snow.

Have you ever seen it?

Outside the box,

where the sun shines upon the snow?

I know you feel your pulse

go by in every moment now,

and you look off the ledge

to see the darkness

down below.

Perception is a tricky thing,

when it seems so doom and gloom,

but perhaps you only see that way

because you are so low?

Perception is a box, you see,

from your eyes unto your brain.

Emotions are but a byproduct

of the thoughts your head has made.

Perception is little box

that grows smaller

when we are low,

but until we look

outside of it

we will never see if

the sun shines upon the snow.

So how can you say

it is the end,

and can you truly know,

if you've never looked

outside that box

to see that sun shines upon the snow?

My point here,

is you are quick to draw,

but not quick to know

that all you feel

is in this box

where you sit with

your fear and woe.

But if you hear

not one more word

to heed before I go,

I would ask that you

remove that box

to the sight of

the sunshine upon the snow."

Stereotype Font

Madman!

Release——

pull up the roots;

bite your tongue——

swallow the blood.

Good!——seal the

deal, pour heart

in the veins. Now

you have it:

A wonderful

display of

caricatures

in stereotype

font. I wonder...

...will they

ever change?

Lithium

Eat the salt in the morning,

it will keep you from flying

up to see the nurses in white.

Happy disposition, you cry

for those weak, weary, hungry,

and alone. You open your

hand, close it, and dream

of stopping their pain———

their ache———

the one deep in your chest.

But the man in the turban

sits at his desk

and offers you a new day———

prescription———

to not see the nurses in white,

but to live your life,

and think your thoughts

differently.

All that can be done

is sit———

perplexed———

with nothing to say...

because you know the salt

will take the sadness away.

Now paper hangs above your bed

to remind you that reality calls

you to fight the voices in your head,

and you weep goodbye yesterday.

You eat the salt at night——

and only sleep remains——

for the rest is a long day

with the venomous salt in your veins.

Mountain Insomniac

The smell of

rain——a tantalizing

concoction,

of sultry

summer heat——

a bastion——

lost within

the screen

of mist that

exudes gray from

the green of the

mountains in

the distance.

Even the

atmosphere

weeps from

time to

time.

Sanguine clouds,

sleepy sun.

We kiss the day

goodnight...

...but the mountains,

they never sleep.

Silence in the Snow

Snow——

a rapture

of sparkling

light, reflected

off of the

crystals the

moon delights,

in pristine

glow———a spectacle

of frigid night———

and man's

life: Inside,

alone:

A captured

heart, held

in the silence

of the snow———

purposeful, a

repose of

figures———

stopped. Frozen.

And staring upward

into the abysmal

night, in wonder

of the world.

Quiet.

Captivated.

A photograph,

as if on a

calendar, with

some word or

wisdom——yet———

that is not

what is here,

in this endless

sky———

for with all

that is spoken

within this moment———

nothing is louder

but the silence of the snow.

Moonbeam (a thought)

The moon,

which lights the darkness,

casts shadows upon the ground.

Red

The sun slits

the sky in

dazzling rays

of red.

The tune she

hears alights

her face

to see a

new tomorrow.

The sky so

red her eyes

behold the

beauty we

all miss———

along the

lines we draw

in the sand,

and see in

black and

white———

but the sun

sets red,

and boils

our blood

as we kiss

the night

a welcome.

And under a

moon——a new,

pristine moon, which

we monotonously

disregard.

Maybe if only

we looked———

we'd see that

even the

sun bleeds

red.

Savanna

The sun bleached

the skies with red

as it doused the

the hills with golden

light——

illuminating the

savanna——

a sight for bright

eyes——

the light of God,

which makes man know

that beauty does exist,

and puts his heart toward

other things——peaceable,

he puts his anger for

his brother away,

and simply enjoys the view.

The Meek Bug

Life is so bleak.

Like a bug,

climbing a vine.

Little does it know,

the sparrow's eye watches

the flower.

A Death

There is a calling in the woods,

for my young heart

longs for the labyrinth

and groves of oak.

A Quiet Morning Walk

Almost sunrise,

but not there yet.

I walk under a

street light to a lake.

The rain falling,

is like weeping

onto the water in little splashes,

quiet explosions——

making a tranquil note,

hitting keys on nature's piano,

a prelude——as the

nocturne slowly dissipates.

There are two ducks—

mallards—

sitting on the water.

and I wonder—

are they sleeping by

programmed instincts?

Waterproof, they don't

concern with the cold that

the rain brings. We are so

different, still I wonder——

could they just be

enjoying the atmosphere like I am?

Mist Kiss of Another Day

The mountains,

kissed by the mist,

is the spectacle

of morning

in which beholding

feels like infinity,

though I know

I have traversed

a day.

A new day is dawning

and clouds plume

beautiful veils of vapor

from the weeping of

the atmosphere.

It covers the mountain

and moves us from

the worries of yesterday.

The Pagan Dance

The green leaves

clothing the trees

tempt my pagan heart

to dance.

My Christened

heart sheds its skin,

and gives in to the labyrinth's

cool stones. Entranced, I walk.

Perhaps to dance

around this path

cures misery because

men were not

meant to live

in tombs with

a window or few.

Thin plates of glass——

like the dissonance

between my mentality

and the trees around me...

...it keeps me dreaming...

...and hoping that

I should even be here,

in this place,

at all.

The Dying Green

In a garden I sat,

close to the house.

Garden green, ever dominant——

it converges upon the oak

and strangles it.

The Labyrinth

Past the village where the farmers sow,

past the forest, to the hillside low,

there is a labyrinth,

in the fields———

where the clovers grow.

End Note

The moon hangs

above the earth,

but no one

looks upon it.

Tell me, have

you forgotten

what makes you man?

Do you not know

why you are?

The moon above,

the eye of God,

sets the torch

in your heart

to dance,

to sing.

Tell me,

why don't you look

upon the moon

and sing a lullaby

to the end

of all things...

About the author

William F. Burk lives in rural Northwest Georgia. Though he began writing at a young age, he didn't seriously begin the art until 2015. He is now the author of several stories, novels, and many poems (most of which are featured in this compendium). Writing is his ultimate passion.

www.ingramcontent.com/pod-product-compliance
Lightning Source LLC
Chambersburg PA
CBHW051807050726
47598CB00006B/2461